THE CIVIL WAR
BLACK SOLDIERS IN THE CIVIL WAR

by Elisabeth Herschbach

FOCUS READERS.

VOYAGER

www.focusreaders.com

Focus Readers is distributed by North Star Editions:
sales@northstareditions.com | 888-417-0195

Produced for Focus Readers by Red Line Editorial.

Content Consultant: Dr. Gideon Mailer, Associate Professor of History, University of Minnesota Duluth

Photographs ©: Everett Historical/Shutterstock Images, cover, 1, 17, 22–23, 28–29, 30, 39; Library of Congress, 4–5, 25, 37, 41, 42–43; Louis Frenzel/Library of Congress, 7; Henry P. Moore/Library of Congress, 8–9; Red Line Editorial, 11, 26; Alma A. Pelot/Library of Congress, 13; Louis N. Rosenthal/Library of Congress, 14–15; C. M. Bell/Library of Congress, 19; Everett Collection Historical/Alamy, 21; W. E. B. DuBois/Library of Congress, 33; Jacob F. Coonley/Library of Congress, 34–35; Launey & Goebel/Library of Congress, 44

Library of Congress Cataloging-in-Publication Data
Names: Herschbach, Elisabeth, author.
Title: Black soldiers in the Civil War / Elisabeth Herschbach.
Description: Lake Elmo : Focus Readers, 2020. | Series: The civil war |
   Includes bibliographical references and index. | Audience: Grades 7-9
Identifiers: LCCN 2019031059 (print) | LCCN 2019031060 (ebook) | ISBN
   9781644930786 (hardcover) | ISBN 9781644931578 (paperback) | ISBN
   9781644933152 (pdf) | ISBN 9781644932360 (ebook)
Subjects: LCSH: United States. Army--African American troops--History--19th
   century--Juvenile literature. | African American soldiers--History--19th
   century--Juvenile literature. | United States--History--Civil War,
   1861-1865--Participation, African American--Juvenile literature.
Classification: LCC E492.9 .H47 2020 (print) | LCC E492.9 (ebook) | DDC
   973.7/415--dc23
LC record available at https://lccn.loc.gov/2019031059
LC ebook record available at https://lccn.loc.gov/2019031060

Printed in the United States of America
Mankato, MN
012020

ABOUT THE AUTHOR

Elisabeth Herschbach is a writer and editor from Washington, DC.

TABLE OF CONTENTS

CHAPTER 1

ESCAPE TO FREEDOM

Elijah P. Marrs crouched in a ditch by the side of the road. He and his companions hid as the rumble of wheels thundered past them. They waited for nearly half an hour. Then, frightened and weary, they continued their 20-mile (32-km) trek through the night.

It was September 25, 1864. A civil war was raging in the United States. Northern states and Southern states were fighting against each other.

Enslaved people fled to camps of the Union army, where they could gain freedom.

Marrs was leading a group of 27 men to freedom. Like Marrs, they had escaped from slavery. Now they were fleeing to Louisville, Kentucky. Once there, they planned to enlist in the Union army to fight on the side of the North.

The men knew how risky their plan was. Runaway slaves were punished severely if they were caught. The men had to travel by night, creeping through woods and along back roads. The journey was difficult and dangerous. But Marrs and the others were determined. Joining the Union army was their best chance of freedom.

As dawn broke on September 26, the exhausted men staggered into Louisville. By eight o'clock in the morning, they reached a recruiting office. Within hours, slaveholders were combing the city streets. They searched for the escaped men. But it was too late. Marrs and his men had already

William Johnson of Kentucky was one of many black men who fought for the Union.

enlisted. And by US law, any slave who enlisted gained emancipation, or freedom from slavery.

Later, Marrs described the experience in a book about his life. He wrote that he could feel freedom in his bones. Even if he died in battle, he would at least die as a free man. And he would be fighting for the freedom of others.

CHAPTER 2

A DIVIDED NATION

The US Civil War broke out in 1861. At that time, approximately four million men, women, and children of African descent lived in the United States as slaves. The vast majority of them lived in the South. In fact, in some Southern states, enslaved people made up more than half of the total population.

Enslaved people had no legal rights. They were forced to work long hours of hard labor.

Plantations in the South depended on enslaved workers to plant and harvest crops.

Many endured harsh treatment, including brutal beatings and whippings. And they were bought and sold like property. All too often, family members were separated.

In the late 1700s, most Northern states began passing laws to gradually end slavery. But slavery remained legal in the South. In fact, the region's economy depended on it. **Plantation** owners used enslaved workers to grow the crops that made them wealthy. Enslaved people were also pressed into service as builders, carpenters, factory workers, and servants. In many Southern states, this unpaid labor accounted for as much as one-third of the income of white people.

Over the decades, disagreements about slavery created deep political divisions between the North and the South. Many Northerners wanted to stop slavery from spreading. Southerners tended to oppose **federal** restrictions on slavery. As the United States expanded westward, conflicts erupted. Many Northerners wanted slavery to be outlawed in the new states and territories. But Southerners didn't want more free states to join the nation. They worried that lawmakers from those states would gain control of Congress.

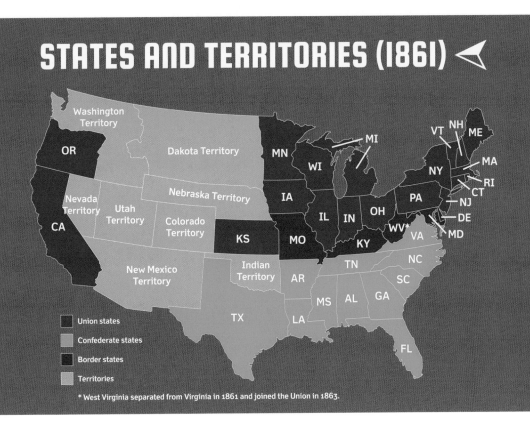

STATES AND TERRITORIES (1861) ◄

Washington Territory

OR

Dakota Territory

MN

WI

MI

VT NH ME

NY MA

RI

CT

Nevada Territory

Utah Territory

Colorado Territory

Nebraska Territory

IA

PA

NJ

DE

CA

KS

MO

IL IN OH

WV*

VA

MD

KY

New Mexico Territory

Indian Territory

AR

TN

NC

SC

MS AL GA

TX

LA

FL

- Union states
- Confederate states
- Border states
- Territories

* West Virginia separated from Virginia in 1861 and joined the Union in 1863.

If that happened, lawmakers might try to ban slavery everywhere in the nation. Without slavery, they feared the South's economy might collapse.

Tensions escalated when Abraham Lincoln was elected president in 1860. Lincoln was a critic of slavery. As a result, he was very unpopular in the South. In December 1860, South Carolina seceded, or officially withdrew, from the United States. Mississippi, Florida, Alabama, Georgia, Louisiana, and Texas soon followed. Together, these states declared themselves a separate country. They called themselves the Confederate States of America.

The crisis turned violent on April 12, 1861. Confederate soldiers attacked Fort Sumter. This Union fort stood in Charleston, South Carolina. The Confederates fired guns and cannons at the fort for two days. Then the Union troops were

▲ Soldiers raise a Confederate flag shortly after taking control of Fort Sumter.

forced to surrender. In response, President Lincoln took action. He called for 75,000 volunteers to enlist in the Union army.

By May, four other states had seceded from the Union and joined the Confederacy. They were Virginia, Arkansas, Tennessee, and North Carolina. The Civil War was in full swing. The nation had splintered into two.

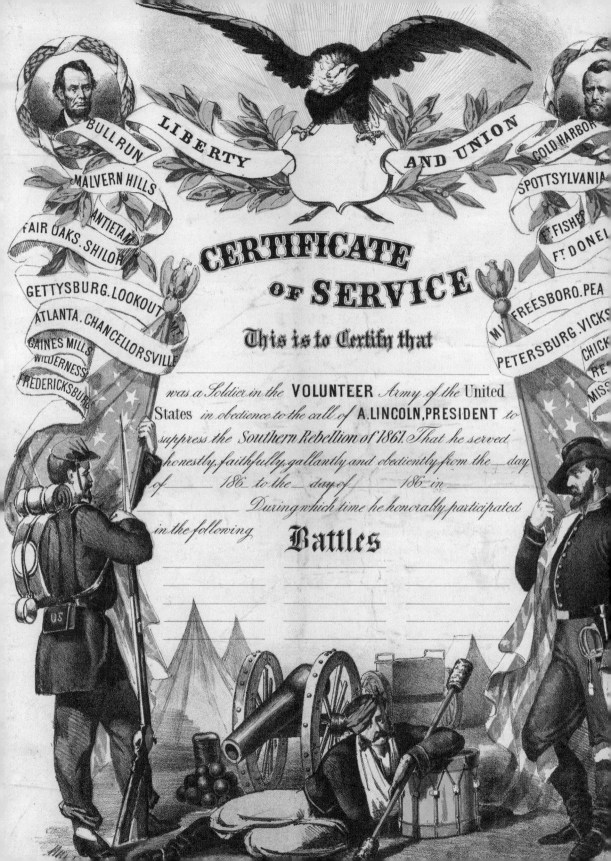

CHAPTER 3

A WHITE MAN'S WAR?

President Lincoln's call for troops got an instant response. Crowds gathered outside army recruitment offices in Northern cities. Marching bands played patriotic songs in the streets. Large numbers of young men, both black and white, rushed to enlist.

When the Civil War began, roughly 200,000 free black people lived in Northern states. Many of them were eager to fight for their country.

People who served in the armed forces were issued a certificate of service.

In fact, black Americans had even more reason than white Americans to serve. They saw military service as a chance to gain more rights for free black people in the North. And they hoped that a Union victory would finally put an end to slavery everywhere in the nation.

Black troops had fought alongside George Washington in the American Revolutionary War (1775–1783). A 1792 law banned black people from joining the army. Even so, black soldiers had served in the War of 1812 (1812–1815). Now, thousands of black Americans were anxious to do their part in the Civil War, too. A black doctor from Michigan volunteered to raise a regiment of five to ten thousand men.

However, for the first two years of the Civil War, the government rejected black volunteers. Lincoln feared public opinion in the border states

⚔ Early in the war, only white men were allowed to serve in the Union army.

of Delaware, Maryland, Kentucky, and Missouri. Slavery was legal in these states. But they had stayed loyal to the Union. Lincoln worried that the border states would see black troops as a threat to slavery. He feared they might secede from the Union and join the Confederacy.

Even in free states, many white people didn't want black soldiers to serve in the military.

Most people expected the war to be over quickly. Recruitment offices had plenty of white volunteers. And although slavery was illegal in most Northern states, racism remained common. Many white people thought black people were inferior. Some felt they weren't capable of being good soldiers. Some simply didn't want to serve alongside them. Others worried that accepting black recruits would increase the number of free black people in the North. They didn't want black workers to compete with white workers for jobs.

Richard Harvey Cain was one of many young black men who tried to enlist. Cain was a student

➤ THINK ABOUT IT

Can you think of another time when public opinion or fears affected a decision made by a government?

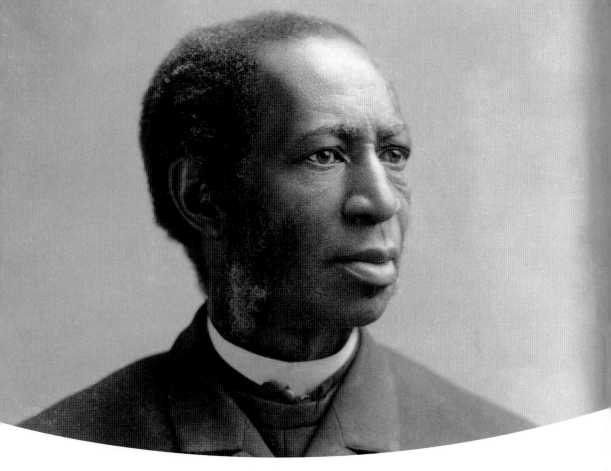

After the Civil War, Richard Harvey Cain served in Congress. He represented the state of South Carolina.

at Wilberforce University in Ohio. He **petitioned** to join the Union army. He told Ohio's governor that more than 100 of his fellow students were also willing to fight. But the governor turned Cain away. This was a white man's war, he said. There was no place for black soldiers in the army.

FREDERICK DOUGLASS

Many black leaders urged President Lincoln to let black Americans serve in the Union army. One of the most vocal was Frederick Douglass. Douglass was an **abolitionist**. As a young man, he escaped from slavery. He became a well-known writer and public speaker.

Douglass believed that fighting for the Union was a way for black men to prove themselves. By risking their lives for their country, they would help convince white people to support their fight for equal rights. Black soldiers would also weaken the South. Seeing black soldiers fight against slavery, Douglass wrote, "would be more terrible than powder and balls."[1]

Douglass argued tirelessly for his views. He wrote to politicians. He gave speeches in cities throughout the North and published a steady stream of newspaper articles. "Let the slaves and

THE NORTH STAR.

RIGHT IS OF NO SEX—TRUTH IS OF NO COLOR—GOD IS THE FATHER OF US ALL, AND ALL WE ARE BRETHREN.

ROCHESTER, N. Y., FRIDAY, JUNE 2, 1848.

WHOLE NO.—23

In the 1840s, Frederick Douglass began an abolitionist newspaper called the *North Star*.

free colored people be called into service, and formed into a liberating army," he wrote. "Every consideration of justice, humanity, and sound policy confirms the wisdom of calling upon black men just now to take up arms in behalf of their country."[2] To Douglass, banning black men from the army was unfair and foolish. Black soldiers could help end the war sooner and save lives.

1. Frederick Douglass. *Frederick Douglass: Selected Speeches and Writings*. Edited by Philip S. Fonor and adapted by Yuval Taylor. Chicago: Lawrence Hill Books, 1999. 449.
2. Douglass. *Selected Speeches and Writings*. 448.

CHAPTER 4

A TURNING POINT

A few black soldiers joined the Confederate army by choice. However, most black people in the Confederate army were enslaved. They dug trenches, repaired equipment, and produced supplies.

In May 1861, some of these enslaved workers escaped. They fled to camps of the Union army. Confederate officers demanded they be sent back. But Union general Benjamin Butler refused.

This man worked as a cook for the Union army.

The Confederate army had paid slaveholders for the slaves' labor. So, Butler reasoned, the enslaved workers were **contraband** of war. He hired them to work for the Union army instead. Later that year, Congress passed the First Confiscation Act, agreeing with Butler's decision.

Enslaved men and women began rushing to Union camps. At first, the camps only accepted people who had worked for Confederate troops. But many Northerners opposed sending anyone back to slavery. By 1862, the camps accepted any enslaved people who reached them. And in July, the Second Confiscation Act stated that anyone who reached Union lines was free.

Escaped slaves often worked in army camps. They helped cook, build, and care for animals. Some also worked as spies and guides. They gave valuable information about Confederate troops.

⚑ Susie King Taylor was the first black woman to serve as an army nurse.

They led Union soldiers through enemy territory. In the process, they often risked their lives. Many black women worked as nurses in army hospitals. They also sewed uniforms, cooked, cleaned, and washed clothes for soldiers.

Meanwhile, the Union army was struggling. Two years into the war, morale in the North was low. The Union had gone into the war expecting an easy win. But the Confederates came out ahead in several early battles. The death toll was mounting.

As the bloody war dragged on, fewer white men wanted to enlist. The Union army struggled to find enough recruits.

Eventually, Lincoln was forced to rethink the ban on black troops. Black men were still eager to serve. Allowing them to fight would give the Union army a big boost. At the same time, Lincoln came to realize the importance of ending slavery.

➤ EARLY CONFEDERATE VICTORIES

July 21, 1861
First Battle of Bull Run

May 25, 1862
First Battle of Winchester

August 28–30, 1862
Second Battle of Bull Run

April 30–May 6, 1863
Battle of Chancellorsville

August 10, 1861
Battle of Wilson's Creek

June 27, 1862
Battle of Gaines's Mill

December 11–15, 1862
Battle of Fredericksburg

Slave labor fueled the Southern war effort, just as it drove the Southern economy. If enslaved people moved North in hope of freedom, the Confederacy would lose a major source of unpaid labor.

On January 1, 1863, Lincoln issued the Emancipation Proclamation. It declared that all enslaved people living in areas fighting against the Union were free. And it authorized the Union army to recruit black soldiers for battle. After a long struggle, black Americans had finally won the right to fight for freedom.

The Emancipation Proclamation marked a turning point in the Civil War. At first, most Northerners had believed the war was only about preserving the Union. Now they were realizing that slavery played a key role, too. Slavery had been one of the causes of the war. And the Union couldn't win without ending this practice.

CHAPTER 5

HEROES ON THE BATTLEFIELD

President Lincoln had no authority over the Confederate states. He could not force Southern slaveholders to set anyone free. Even so, the Emancipation Proclamation had a huge impact. Enslaved people had been escaping to Union land since the start of the war. But the Emancipation Proclamation inspired more people to run away than ever before. Many escaped to Union camps and joined the army.

These men drove wagons that carried supplies for the Union army.

A Union soldier stands with a group of people who lived on a plantation in South Carolina.

Historians estimate that as many as 700,000 enslaved people escaped to Union lines during the war. This was a crippling loss for the Confederacy. For the Union, it was a major gain. Its army gained many new soldiers and workers.

By enlisting, black people gained their freedom. They also helped spread freedom to others. When Union troops conquered Confederate territory, enslaved people in that area were set free.

In total, approximately 198,000 black men fought for the Union. The majority were formerly enslaved. But many free black people from the North also served in the military. In fact, there were so many black recruits that the government needed a special department to manage them. This department was called the Bureau of Colored Troops. It began operating in May 1863.

One of the first black units to form was the 54th Massachusetts Regiment. This unit started recruiting in February 1863, just one month after Lincoln signed the Emancipation Proclamation. By May, 1,000 men had enlisted. That number included men from 24 different states.

The Massachusetts 54th faced its first major test in July 1863. Six hundred men from the regiment were chosen to lead an assault against Fort Wagner. This fort stood on Morris Island.

Along with Fort Sumter, it played a key role in defending the city of Charleston.

The men marched through stormy weather for miles before the battle. They went two days without food or sleep. Worse still, they were badly outnumbered. Nearly three times as many Confederate soldiers defended the fort.

Despite all this, the 54th fought heroically. One soldier ran through gunfire to protect the Union flag. His name was William H. Carney. Sergeant Carney was shot many times. But he never let the flag drop. He became the first black soldier to win the Medal of Honor. This is the US military's highest honor.

> ## THINK ABOUT IT

Why do you think the story of the Massachusetts 54th got so much attention?

▲ William H. Carney received the Medal of Honor in 1900.

In the end, the 54th was defeated. Nearly half the men were captured, hurt, or killed. But stories of their bravery spread. They demonstrated that black men could be great soldiers.

CHAPTER 6

SEPARATE AND UNEQUAL

For the next two years, black soldiers fought in many battles. In fact, by the end of the war, black Union troops had taken part in nearly 450 military actions. More than 40 of these were major battles. Sixteen black soldiers received the Medal of Honor. And approximately 37,000 died for the Union cause.

Historians today recognize the important role these black soldiers played in the Union's victory.

Members of the Tennessee Colored Battery camp at Johnsonville, Tennessee.

At the time, however, black soldiers didn't receive the respect they deserved. In many cases, they had to fight a war on two fronts. One enemy was the Confederate army. The other was discrimination within the Union army.

Black and white troops could not serve in the same units. Instead, the Union army put black soldiers in **segregated** regiments. White officers were in charge of many of these all-black units.

Black soldiers were paid less, too. White **privates** received $13 a month. An extra $3 was added on for clothing. White officers earned even more. But regardless of their rank, black soldiers received only $7 a month, plus the $3 for clothing.

Many black soldiers were outraged. They held protests and petitioned the government. They wrote letters to newspapers. Several regiments refused to accept any pay at all unless they were

⚠ Black soldiers earned less pay to send home to their families than white soldiers.

paid as much as white soldiers. Finally, in June 1864, Congress passed a law granting equal pay to black soldiers.

Black soldiers faced many other kinds of unfair treatment. Compared to white troops, black soldiers received worse equipment. Their uniforms were often shabby and poorly made.

Their weapons were old and sometimes defective. And in many cases, they did not receive good training.

White soldiers spent most of their time training, resting, or fighting. By contrast, black regiments were assigned long hours of hard labor known as fatigue duty. This work included difficult and unpleasant jobs such as digging trenches, building roads, cleaning out toilets, and burying corpses. After working all day, black troops had little time left for training. As a result, they were often poorly prepared for battle.

Many soldiers protested. But the government did not take action until June 1864. After that, commanders were required to keep all soldiers' fatigue duty equal. However, the new rule proved hard to enforce. Some commanders continued to burden black soldiers with extra work.

Members of the 29th Connecticut Volunteer Infantry train by performing a drill in 1864.

The lack of good weapons and training cost many black soldiers their lives. Poor medical care claimed even more. Hospitals for black soldiers were often unclean and did not have enough workers. Many white doctors refused to care for black patients. And there was a shortage of black doctors. By the war's end, disease had killed more than twice as many black soldiers as white soldiers.

WILLIAM WELLS BROWN

If captured, black soldiers faced great danger. They could be sold into slavery or brutally killed. One of the most notorious examples happened at Fort Pillow, Tennessee. Approximately 550 Union soldiers defended the fort. Roughly half of them were black. On April 12, 1864, Confederates captured the fort and killed two-thirds of the black soldiers. Only one-third of white defenders died.

Confederates claimed the black soldiers fought back. But people in the North believed it was a deliberate **massacre**. For example, William Wells Brown called the events "a horrid butchery."[1]

Brown had escaped from slavery in Tennessee. He became a well-known abolitionist, historian, and writer. Brown wrote about the attack in 1867. He described how the Union soldiers "held up

▲ Confederate soldiers shot and killed black defenders during an infamous attack on Fort Pillow, Tennessee.

their hands, and begged their captors to spare their lives."[2] Instead, the Confederates shot them.

Although the details are debated, eyewitnesses agree that some black soldiers were executed. Brown believed these brutal actions reflected the cruelty of slavery. He wrote: "In no other school than slavery could human beings have been trained to such readiness for cruelties like these."[3]

1. William Wells Brown. *The Negro in the American Rebellion.* Boston: Lee & Shepard, 1867. 235.
2. Brown. *The Negro in the American Rebellion.* 241.
3. Brown. *The Negro in the American Rebellion.* 235.

CHAPTER 7

FREE AT LAST

Union troops captured Charleston in February 1865. Four years earlier, the first shots of the Civil War had been fired there. Now, two black regiments had the honor of leading the march into the city. Charleston's black residents poured into the streets. They cheered and greeted the soldiers as heroes. By April, the war had officially ended.

After they returned home, black **veterans** often took on leadership roles in their communities.

Soldiers prepare to raise the US flag at Fort Sumter on April 14, 1865.

This family lived in Savannah, Georgia, in the late 1800s.

Many had gained new skills in the army. And with the money they had earned, they could invest in a better future. Some bought land. Others paid for schooling or started businesses. Elijah P. Marrs, for example, became a pastor and teacher. He and his brother founded a university.

For black veterans who returned to the South, life could be very hard. They suffered threats, harassment, and violent attacks. Many became field-workers or **sharecroppers** on the plantations where they had been enslaved. They earned very little money. But they did gain freedom. In 1865, the Thirteenth **Amendment** to the US Constitution took effect. Slavery was outlawed nationwide.

Other important changes soon followed. In 1868, the Fourteenth Amendment affirmed that black Americans were citizens. It said they were entitled to equal protection under the law. And in 1870, the Fifteenth Amendment gave black men the right to vote. The Civil War had ended, but the fight for civil rights was just beginning.

THINK ABOUT IT ◄

Many black veterans of the Civil War later became leaders in the fight for civil rights. How might their experiences in the Union army have prepared them for that role?

FOCUS ON
BLACK SOLDIERS IN THE CIVIL WAR

Write your answers on a separate piece of paper.

1. Write a paragraph describing some of the inequality black soldiers in the Union army faced.

2. Do you think the Union army should have accepted black recruits earlier on in the war? Why or why not?

3. Which document allowed black soldiers to serve in the Union army?
    - **A.** the Thirteenth Amendment
    - **B.** the Fourteenth Amendment
    - **C.** the Emancipation Proclamation

4. Why did the Emancipation Proclamation motivate more enslaved people to escape?
    - **A.** It showed the Union would support their cause.
    - **B.** It meant they would no longer have to travel as far.
    - **C.** It meant they could no longer be captured and sent back.

Answer key on page 48.

GLOSSARY

abolitionist
A person who wants to end slavery.

amendment
A change or addition to a legal document.

contraband
Property captured from enemy troops.

federal
Having to do with the top level of government, involving the whole nation rather than just one state.

massacre
The violent killing of many people.

petitioned
Sent a formal request for change, often one signed by many people, to a higher authority.

plantation
A large farm where crops such as cotton, sugar, or tobacco are grown.

privates
The lowest-ranking soldiers in the military.

segregated
Separate or set apart based on race, sex, or religion.

sharecroppers
Farmers who rent land from its owner and give a share of their crops in exchange for working the land.

veterans
People who have served in the military.

TO LEARN MORE

BOOKS

Cornell, Kari A. *African Americans in the Civil War.* Minneapolis: Abdo Publishing, 2017.

Randolph, Joanne, ed. *African American Soldiers.* New York: Enslow Publishing, 2018.

Shepard, Ray Anthony. *Now or Never! 54th Massachusetts Infantry's War to End Slavery.* Honesdale, PA: Highlights, 2017.

NOTE TO EDUCATORS

Visit **www.focusreaders.com** to find lesson plans, activities, links, and other resources related to this title.

INDEX

Answer Key: 1. Answers will vary; **2.** Answers will vary; **3.** C; **4.** A